WHAT·DO·WE·KNOW ABOUT THE EGYPTIANS?

JOANNA·DEFRATES

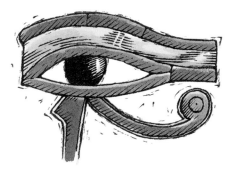

PETER BEDRICK BOOKS

NEW YORK

First American edition published
in 1992 by
Peter Bedrick Books
2112 Broadway
New·York, NY 10023

Library of Congress Cataloging-in-Publication Data
Defrates, Joanna.
   What do we know about the
Egyptians?/Joanna Defrates.
   1st American ed.
   Includes index.
   Summary: An illustrated survey of
ancient Egypt's history, religion,
and sociology.
   ISBN 0–87226–353–3
   1. Egypt – Civilization – To
332 B.C. – Juvenile literature.
   [1. Egypt – Civilization – To
332 B.C.]   I. Title.
   DT61.D37   1992
   932′.01–dc20   91–25175
                           CIP
Reprinted in 1994   AC

Design: David West
         Children's Book Design

Illustrator: Rob Shone

Editor: Ros Mair

Photograph acknowledgements:
Ashmoleum, Oxford: 17 (t); Peter
Clayton: 9 (l), 12, 13 (b), 15 (b), 16, 19, 20,
21 (b), 25 (b), 26, 30, 31 (b), 33 (t) (b),
34 (l) (r), 40–1, 42, 43; Joanna
Defrates: 8, 9 (r), 13, 15, 19 (r), 21, 22,
23 (t), 28, 29, 36, 37, 38, 39 (l);
C M Dixon: 14, 35 (tr) (br);
George Hart: 31 (t); Michael Holford:
Cover, 17 (br), 23 (b), 24, 25 (t), 27, 32,
35 (l), 39 (br); British Museum: endpages;
Cover: Hunefer and his wife Nasha

Picture research: Joanna Defrates and
                     Jennie Karrach

Typeset by: Goodfellow and Egan,
Cambridge

Printed and bound by Paramount
Printing Group Ltd., Hong Kong

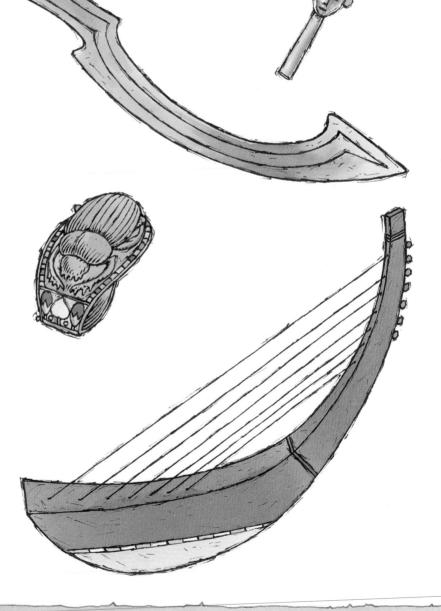

· CONTENTS ·

WHO·WERE·THE·EGYPTIANS?

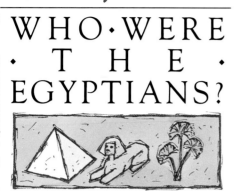

About 10,000 years ago, after the last Ice Age, the valley of the Nile became the center of one of the world's greatest civilizations. People began to settle along the narrow strip of fertile land (rarely more than 12 miles) beside the river. The yearly flood brought thick, black silt to cover the fields. Food was easy to grow. There was plenty of spare time to develop art and crafts, literature and music. Egypt was secure, surrounded by deserts on three sides and protected by invaders from across the sea by muddy marshes. Egyptians were very grateful that they did not live "abroad".

PAPYRUS AND LOTUS

The two symbols of Egypt are the papyrus, representing the delta marshes, and the lotus, representing the river valley.

TWO LANDS

The Egyptians saw their land in two parts: Upper Egypt (the valley) and Lower Egypt (the delta). Unfortunately, we know little about the delta in ancient times – the level of the water has risen which means most of the early settlements are deeply buried in mud and silt. The ruler of Egypt was called "Lord of the Two Lands".

THE RIVERSIDE

The people called their land *Kemi*, meaning the Black Land which is the color of the soil, while the desert was known as *Desret* – the Red Land. As a famous Greek traveler wrote, "Egypt is the gift of the Nile". Sometimes the fertile land is only one mile wide, and the desert comes down almost to the water's edge.

WHAT DID THE EGYPTIANS LOOK LIKE?

It is difficult to say exactly what a typical Egyptian adult looked like, but they were fairly short, about 5 ft 5 inches, and slightly built with straight black hair, dark eyes and copper colored skin. Later on many people settled in Egypt from both the north and the south. As long as they adopted Egyptian ways and culture, they were thought of as Egyptian.

PRINCE RAHOTEP AND HIS WIFE NOFRET

This Egyptian couple lived about 4,000 years ago. Nofret wears a wig while her husband has a fashionable moustache.

HOW DO WE KNOW?

For a long time Egypt was seen as a land of mystery and magic. No one even knew what a pyramid was for. But just over a hundred years ago, a brilliant young French scholar deciphered the Egyptian language. The symbols, known as hieroglyphs, can be read like any other written language.

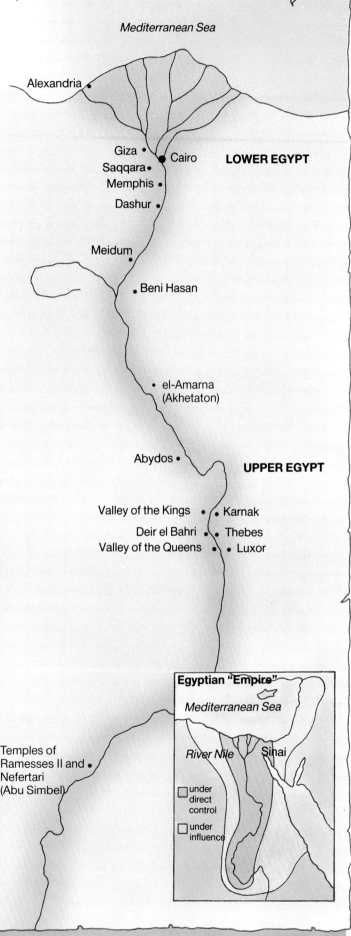

Mediterranean Sea

Alexandria

Giza
Saqqara
Cairo
LOWER EGYPT
Memphis

Dashur

Meidum

Beni Hasan

el-Amarna
(Akhetaton)

Abydos
UPPER EGYPT

Valley of the Kings • • Karnak
Deir el Bahri • • Thebes
Valley of the Queens • • Luxor

Temples of
Ramesses II and •
Nefertari
(Abu Simbel)

Egyptian "Empire"

Mediterranean Sea

River Nile   Sinai

☐ under
direct
control

☐ under
influence

TIMELINE

	BC 3000	2700	2400	2100	1800	1500
EVENTS IN EGYPT	Unification of Egypt. Development of art and writing. **Double crown**	Step Pyramid built. Imhotep as King's Chancellor. Rahotep and Nofret lived. Hesire as Chief Doctor and Dentist. Building of the Pyramids and Sphinx. Seneb and his family at court.	First obelisks built. Highly decorated tombs for nobles.	End of the Old Kingdom. Queen Kawit ruled (c.2030). Middle Kingdom (c.2000 BC). Meserheti's wooden model soldiers.	Smaller pyramids built of brick were built surrounded by planned towns. The King as a good shepherd often shown worried and careworn. Collapse of Middle Kingdom.	Rise of New Kingdom. Deir el Bahri built. Huge new temples at Karnak and Luxor dedicated to Amun. A new capital at Amarna – this is abandoned after 20 years. Tutankhamun moves the court back to Thebes.
PHARAOHS AND RULERS	Narmer or Menes – who united Egypt. **King Narmer**	The great pyramid builders: Djoser (builder of the Step Pyramid), Sneferu, Khufu, Khafre and Menkaure.	Unas – the first pharaoh to have inscriptions inside his pyramid. Pepi – ruled for over 90 years. First queen to rule.	'70 kings who ruled for 70 days' a slight exaggeration but a time of internal revolt. Mentuhotep – a prince of Thebes reunited the country (his temple is next to Hatshepsut's at Deir el Bahri).	Time of the great pharaohs of the Middle Kingdom like Senwosret and Amenemhat. This period also ended with a ruling queen. Followed by invasion by foreigners called Hyksos.	Egypt re-united under a Theban prince again. The great 18th dynasty. Tuthmosis III – he was only about 5' tall, his aunt and stepmother Hatshepsut, Amenophis III, his grandson Tutankhamun, and Queen Nefertiti.
CONQUESTS	Possible contacts with the eastern Mediterranean and the Red Sea.	Trade with Lebanon and Byblos. Trade all the way into Somalia.	Expeditions into Nubia and the Sudan.	Collapse of Old Kingdom. Independence of local princes. Many petty kings. **Scimitar**	Conquest of Nubia. Great fortresses built.	Egypt invaded by Hyksos – foreign princes from the north but eventually Egypt expelled them. Expeditions to the Euphrates. Re-took Nubia. Annexed Syria and Palestine. Greatest expansion of Egypt.
EVENTS AROUND THE WORLD	Growth of towns in Mesopatamia. Invention of writing. Egyptian contact with Palestine. Long barrows in Britain. **Stonehenge**	Royal cemetery at Ur. First period of Stonehenge. First metal objects of copper found in Britain.	Growth of Mohenjo-Daro the great city of the Indus civilization in Pakistan. They traded all the way to the Mediterranean.	Last period of Stonehenge. Rise of Babylon.	Growth of Hittite empire in Asia. Rule of the Minoans in Crete. Palace of Knosses built.	Rise of Mycenae in Greece. Santorini erupts. Minoan civilization collapses.

1200	900	600	300	AD
Pleated linen is fashionable. Tombs are often painted yellow. Sennedjem lived at Deir el Medina. Abu Simbel built.	New Kingdom ended.	Old styles copied in art.	Alexandria founded. Many new temples built (most are still standing).	Roman nobles forbidden to visit Egypt without special permission. It becomes a land of mystery and magic. Some Egyptians become Christians known as Copts.

Cleopatra

1200	900	600	300	AD
A new family from the Delta ruled. There were at least 11 Ramesses but the famous ones are Ramesses II (the Great) and III.	Power split between princes in the Delta and the High Priest of Amun at Thebes. Libyan kings ruled in the Delta. Ethiopian kings rule.	Cambyses – the Persian invaded Egypt c.400. Nectanebo, the last Egyptian Pharoah.	Egypt a Persian province again. Alexander of Macedon conquers Egypt. Ptolemy I as Pharaoh. Cleopatra was defeated by Rome.	Ruled by Roman Emperors. Trajan and Hadrian visited Egypt. They are shown in Pharaohic dress with their names in cartouches.

1200	900	600	300	AD
Lost power in Syria and Palestine War against Hittites in Syria. Both sides claimed a victory.	No more conquests or expansion.	Thebes sacked by Assyrians (663 BC)		

Chariot

1200	900	600	300	AD
Hittite empire falls. Mycenae destroyed. Expansion of nomadic tribes from Asia.	Assyrian empire. Kingdoms of Israel and Judah. Beginning of the Olympic games.	Collapse of Nineveh. Celtic peoples in Britain. Jerusalem destroyed by Nebuchanezzar. Greek expansion.	Alexander the Great reaches India. Greeks and Persians at war. Rise of Rome.	Roman Empire (including England and France).

Alexander the Great

PERIODS OF EGYPTIAN HISTORY

Egyptian history has been divided by historians into different periods. The Egyptians did not use these names – they dated their years from the first year of each new ruler.

Predynastic Egypt
5000–3100 BC
Early Dynastic
Old Kingdom
c.2500–2100
1 Intermediate Period
Middle Kingdom
c.2000–1650
2 Intermediate Period
New Kingdom
c.1550–1100
3 Intermediate Period
Late period c.700–332
Graeco-Roman Period
332–395 AD

An early historian put the Egyptian rulers into 32 families or *dynasties* and that is the name we still use. It is very difficult to be exact about many dates, so we say "circa", meaning about.

BC or AD?
This book was first published in 1991. Another way of writing the date is AD 1991. Our dates are taken from the year Christ was born. The letters AD stand for *Anno Domini* which means "in the year of our Lord". The years before Christ (BC) are counted backwards – look at the timeline.

D I D · T H E EGYPTIANS · G R O W · THEIR · OWN · F O O D ?

REAPING
Here we see Sennedjem cutting corn with a wooden sickle set with flint teeth. Right behind him is his wife carrying a basket. This painting is taken from Sennedjem's tomb and shows an idealized view of harvesting. The couple are dressed in their very best clothes and wigs which would not really happen at harvest-time!

It was the yearly flood that gave Egypt its rich farming land. The floods spread over the valley in the summer when it was almost too hot to work. By October the ground was covered by a thick layer of black silt, ready for the farmers to plow and sow with crops like barley, flax and wheat. Barley was used to make bread and beer, the staple diet of the poor, and flax was woven into fine linen clothes. All crops were assessed for taxes. Small boys scared away the birds from the young grain and when it was harvest-time everybody joined in to help. The very poor were allowed to glean what the harvesters had left behind. The land was so fertile that it was even possible to grow two crops a year.

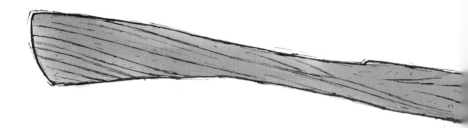

PLOW

Light wooden plows turned the soil. They were pulled by cattle, or even men.

Plow

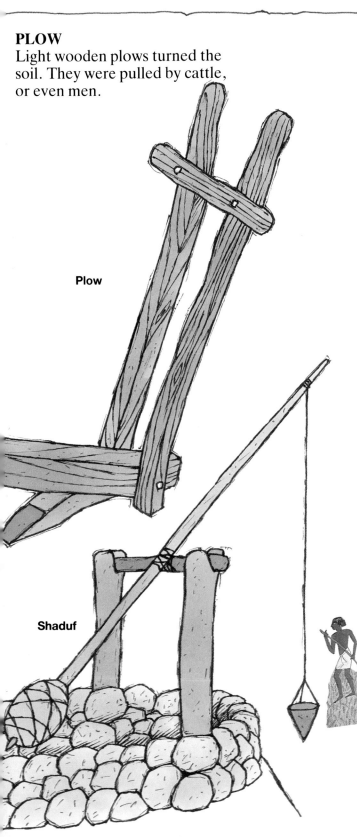

Shaduf

SHADUF

As the level of the fields was above the Nile they had to be irrigated. Farmers developed a device we call a shaduf. By using a counterweight at the end of a long pole, buckets of water could be lifted.

THE LAND

Three thousand years ago an Egyptian wrote a poem about his home: *"Its fields are full of good things and it has provision for every day. Its granaries overflow . . . they reach the sky. Its ponds are full of fishes and its lakes of birds. Its fields are green with grass and its banks bear dates. He who lives there is happy and the poor man is like the great elsewhere".*

CATTLE

Exact records of numbers and owners of cattle were kept for tax purposes. There were at least three different breeds, including one with long, sharp horns. Wild bulls were also hunted for sport and an ox-leg is often shown as a tomb offering.

FARMERS

Farmers never used horses on the land. They were too valuable. The building of the Aswan Dam has stopped the yearly floods. This means that today's farmers have to add extra fertilizer to the once-rich soil.

DID·THE EGYPTIANS EAT·WELL?

The Egyptians loved good food and drink. They often ate so much at banquets that they made themselves sick! Even poor people had a healthy diet of vegetables, bread and fruit as well as fish from the Nile. Meat was roasted and stewed with herbs and spices. The only imported food was olive oil from Syria and a few special spices. Food was eaten with the fingers, but in well-to-do houses there was always a servant carrying scented water and a napkin.

EATING AND DRINKING

In a very hot climate preserving food is important. Duck and fish were dried in the sun, although fish was often salted too as you can see in the ancient wall relief on the facing page. The main source of protein was bread. As a little sand was often added to the flour to help grind it, the gritty result was very bad for the teeth and even kings suffered from toothache. The national drink was beer, made from barley like the bread. Richer people drank wine which was stored in clay jars. Cheap wine was often labeled "for tax purposes only" on the clay jar. There were many wine bars and taverns but no public restaurants as far as we know. Young men were often warned about drinking too much.

COUNTING THE GEESE

A scribe on the left counts the eggs as well as the geese, while the herdsmen bow before their master.

TIGER NUT SWEETS

The Egyptians loved sweet things. Bakers made many different types of bread and rolls, often sweetened with nuts and honey. This recipe was especially popular.

Blend 7 ounces of fresh dates with a little water. Add a little cinnamon and cardamom to taste and coarsely chopped walnuts. Shape into balls, then coat in honey and ground almonds.

EGYPTIAN FOOD AND DRINK

Lentils	Ox
Beans	Wine
Cucumber	Beer
Onions	Milk
Lettuce	Dates
Leeks	Figs
Garlic	Melons
Fish	Grapes
Duck	Pomegranates
Geese	Honey was used for sweetening

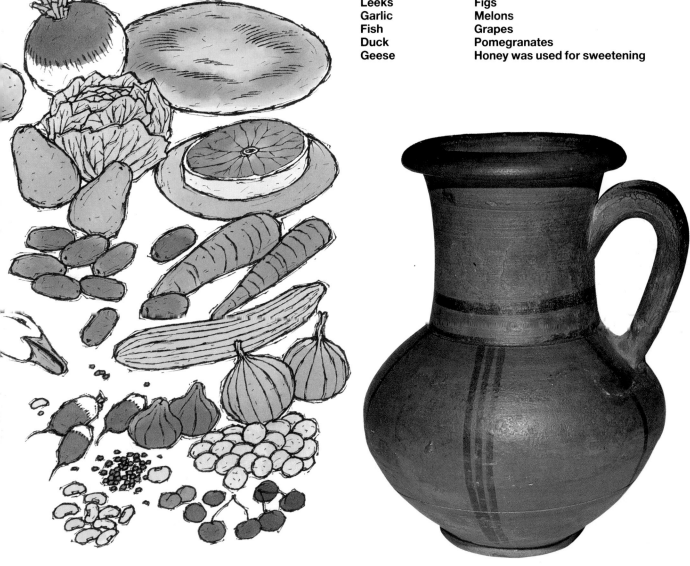

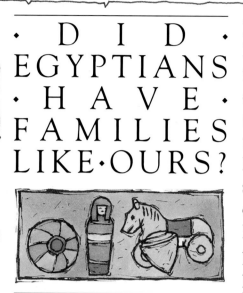

· D I D · EGYPTIANS · H A V E · FAMILIES LIKE·OURS?

Egyptian families were very much like ours, but larger. It was usual to marry young and have many children as the death rate was high and children meant wealth. Sons carried on the family profession. Boys were often named after their grandfathers, and some continued to live with their parents even after marriage. The head of the household had responsibility for unmarried aunts and sisters so it is difficult to know how many people lived in one house. Girls stayed at home until they got married. Divorce was legal but costly. Although women owned property and made their own wills, they took little part in public affairs and were really under their father's or husband's control. But we know of many long and happy marriages with lots of affection between parents and children.

MARRIAGE

Marriage was often within the same family. Uncles married nieces and cousins married cousins. A richer household had many servants who were foreigners captured in war. Sometimes they even married into the family.

THE FOREMAN'S FAMILY

Below is Inhirkha, his wife, son and grandchildren. He was a foreman working on the king's tomb in temperatures of over 100°F. Although a grandfather, he is shown in the prime of life while his grandchildren play with their pet birds around his chair. Even though this is a tomb-painting, it is a happy celebration of family life.

YOUNG PRINCESSES
Two of the six daughters of Queen Nefertiti sitting on an embroidered cushion. This is part of a much larger painting and the sisters are sitting at their mother's heel. The girls are drawn in the style of the time.

Women gave birth kneeling on special bricks.

Girls married at about 12, boys at 14. The average lifetime was about 40, although one king ruled for 96 years and another for 67!

TOYS AND GAMES
Childhood was short but there were lots of toys, and games to play like leapfrog and statues. Boys and girls played with dolls, balls, spinning tops and wooden animals, as well as knucklebones and board games.

PETS
Some children had a monkey or a gazelle as a pet, but cats and dogs were more usual. Cats were sacred and are often shown with a gold earring. Dogs were used in hunting and also by the army and police.

Ball

Wooden horse

Wooden lion

Knucklebone

DID · THE EGYPTIANS LIVE · IN · HOUSES?

Temples for worshipping the gods were built of stone, so that they would last forever, but other buildings in Egypt were made of whitewashed mud-brick. This is the main reason why so few ordinary houses have survived. There were two types of private house – those in the town and those in the country. Town houses had two or three stories with doors opening onto the narrow dusty streets. So, if they could afford it, many people preferred to live on country estates surrounded by gardens and shaded pools.

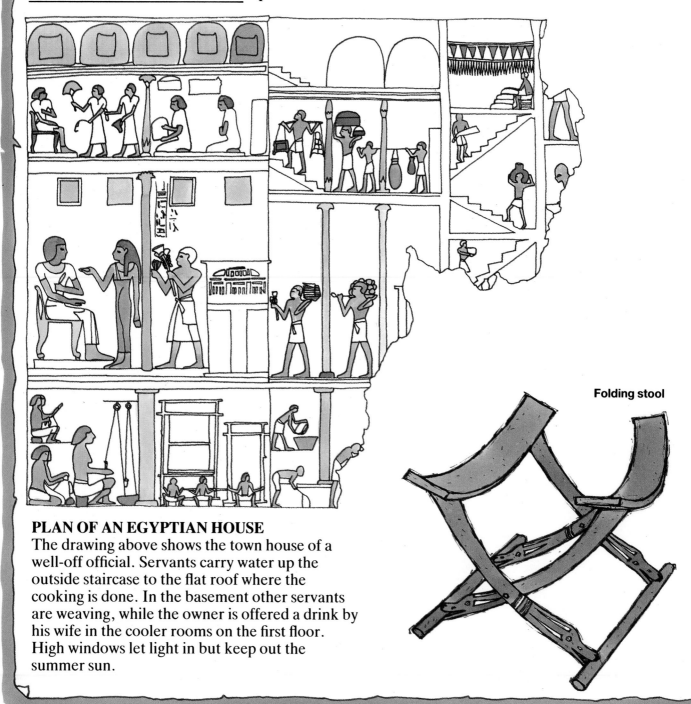

Folding stool

PLAN OF AN EGYPTIAN HOUSE
The drawing above shows the town house of a well-off official. Servants carry water up the outside staircase to the flat roof where the cooking is done. In the basement other servants are weaving, while the owner is offered a drink by his wife in the cooler rooms on the first floor. High windows let light in but keep out the summer sun.

FURNITURE

Houses were not filled with furniture. Those who could afford it used low chairs and tables. Folding stools with legs carved in the form of birds and animals were very popular. Chair seats were made of wood or leather, but servants and poorer people squatted on brightly colored mats or cushions.

Oil lamp on stand

Three-legged table

Headrest

Chair

HOW DO WE KNOW?

Evidence on what sort of houses the Egyptians lived in comes mainly from tomb-paintings and models found in the tombs. However, archaeological excavations are giving us more and more information. Often, though, it is difficult to dig up evidence as new villages are built on top of old ones. The excavated village below was officially built for the workers on the royal tombs and was occupied for more than 300 years. Each house was about 16 × 50 feet with a flat roof and a small yard. You can see that most of the houses opened onto the main street.

A COUNTRY HOUSE

The house on the left belonged to an official called Nakht. The roof towers would catch any breeze. Trees like the sycamore, fig and acacia were grown for fruit and shade.

POPULATION

The capital city, Memphis, had a population of about 500,000.

The total population of Egypt might have been as high as 4 million, with about six people to each house.

· D I D · CHILDREN GO · TO ·SCHOOL?·

THE SCRIBE
Hesire sits with his brush, water-pot and palette over his shoulder. He was Chief Dentist and Doctor as well as a scribe (rather like a civil servant).

We know little about Egyptian schools as there are no pictures of teaching. The Egyptians were more interested in the results of education than in how it was achieved. Some of the temples had boarding schools attached to them known as "houses of instruction". Boys were sometimes sent to "wise men" as pupils, and the sons of high officials were brought up at the royal court. Literacy and a good education were very important and becoming a scribe opened the way to all the professions, such as medicine, the civil service and the priesthood.

Girls did not go to school but were taught at home. They learned all the household skills and, there is evidence that many could also read and write. Poorer children followed their parents' work by helping in the fields or looking after the animals.

STUDYING
Reading was learned by chanting aloud, beginning with whole words and phrases, not with individual letters. Model letters were copied out onto flakes of limestone (papyrus was too expensive for small boys to practise on). Arithmetic was worked out silently. They calculated in 10s, but had no separate numbers for 2 to 9. So 35 was written as
$10+10+10+1+1+1+1+1$.

$10 = \cap$

$1 = |$

$100 = \mathcal{C}$

$1000 = ?$

So $42 = $ ∩∩|
∩∩|

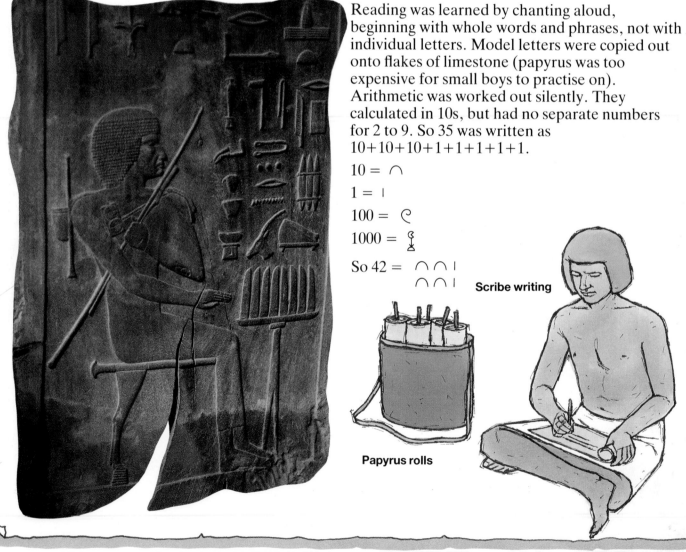

Scribe writing

Papyrus rolls

Scribe's brush-holder and writing equipment

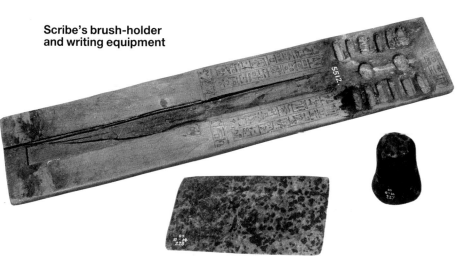

Hieroglyph is a Greek word meaning "sacred writing in stone".

The papyrus plant grows to about 13 feet high.

Papyrus plant

LETTERS
Writing was more like painting with the reed pen held above the paper. It was still simpler than carving the words in stone as in the picture below.

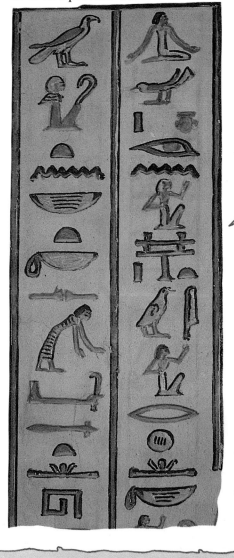

LANGUAGE
The Ancient Egyptian language has an alphabet of 23 letters plus about 700 other phonetic signs (representing sounds). It can be read from left to right, right to left or vertically depending on the way the signs face. Only the consonants are shown, not the vowels, and there are no full-stops. Signs show where a word ends. For everyday business a different script was used, more like our modern handwriting. Letters were written together and not written out as separate signs.

MAKING PAPER
Strips of the inner papryus reed were laid in vertical and horizontal layers and squashed by pressure into a single sheet. This was polished and smoothed to make "paper". Sheets were fixed together to form a roll rather than a book. Papyrus could even be cleaned and re-used. Much of our information about the Egyptian religion has come from rolls of papyrus found in tombs.

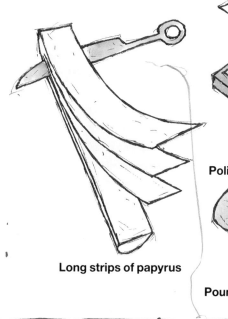

Long strips of papyrus

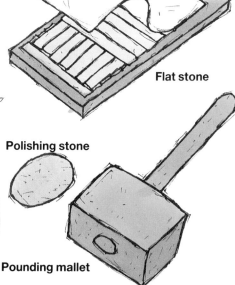

Cover cloth

Flat stone

Polishing stone

Pounding mallet

WHO·WENT TO·WORK· IN·ANCIENT ·EGYPT?·

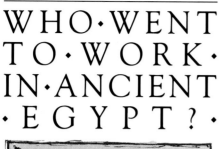

Since the whole of Egypt belonged to the Pharaoh, everybody in it worked for him. In real life, thousands of craftsmen worked for government officials or the temples. Just as today big building projects need stonemasons, carpenters, architects, decorators, floor-layers and painters, so too did the monuments of ancient Egypt. The huge pyramids and temples required an army of laborers as well as specialist craftsmen. Unskilled forced labor was used at the time of the Nile floods, in the summer.

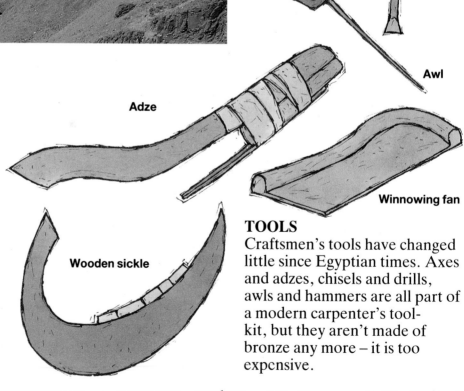

Bow drill

Chisel

Awl

Adze

Winnowing fan

Wooden sickle

TEMPLE OF DEIR EL-BAHRI
This is still one of the most spectacular temples in Egypt. It is built under a natural pyramid – the mountain itself – and originally had gardens and trees in the front and was brightly painted. Along the upper terrace were rows of statues of Queen Hatshepsut. This was her mortuary temple. She was daughter of one king and widow of another and stepmother to a third. As Pharaoh she herself ruled for over 20 years. She ordered the building of the obelisk which you can see on page 39.

TOOLS
Craftsmen's tools have changed little since Egyptian times. Axes and adzes, chisels and drills, awls and hammers are all part of a modern carpenter's tool-kit, but they aren't made of bronze any more – it is too expensive.

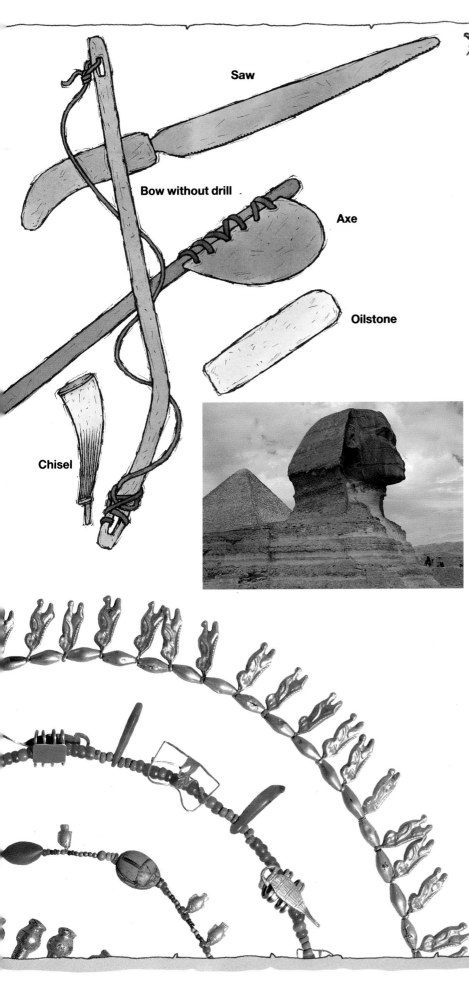

Saw

Bow without drill

Axe

Oilstone

Chisel

WORKMEN

Workmen in the Royal Tombs worked an 8-day week, an 8-hour day with an hour off for lunch. The excuses for not working were many and varied.

The first recorded strikes in history took place over 3,000 years ago. The workmen sat in the shade and refused to work until all their back rations were paid.

SPHINX

Carved from natural rock over 4,500 years ago , the sphinx has the body of a lion and the face of a man – probably King Khafre whose pyramid it guards. Perhaps this could be called one of the world's first "portraits"?

ECONOMICS

The Egyptians had no word for shop or merchant, but people did exchange goods for others of equal value. Profit was not important at all and there was no actual money, but people knew the value of every article. For example, a donkey and two pairs of sandals might equal five sheets and a sack of corn.

JEWELERY

Jewelery-making was a very specialized craft. Workers in gold, lapis lazuli, semi-precious stones and beads shared the same premises but all had special titles. Stone beads were drilled and highly polished, while gold beads were usually made in two halves and soldered together. In the picture you can see many different types of bead necklaces.

· W H A T · · D I D · T H E · EGYPTIANS · D O · O N · · T H E I R · HOLIDAYS?

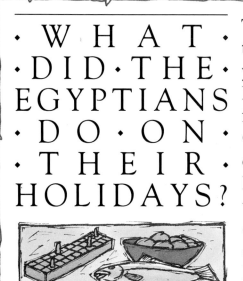

HUNTING

Even more popular than hunting was fishing and fowling. Professionals used traps and nets, but the amateur showed his skill with a throw stick. Here, Nebamun brings down a duck which his cat retrieves. His family watch, dressed in their best clothing. As this is a tomb painting, it is an idealized picture of hunting. Ladies did not go fishing wearing perfume cones and their most fashionable wigs!

The Egyptians did not have annual holidays like us, but there were many festivals and "holydays" through the year – the festival of the god Amun lasted a month. Eventually, holidays were about one third of the year, so for most people there was plenty of time for leisure. One of the favorite pastimes for the well-off was hunting, either out in the desert or in the delta marshes. After the horse and chariot were introduced, lion hunts became very popular. Skill in horsemanship was admired, and one king boasted how he had killed seven lions and captured a herd of wild cattle before breakfast! The Egyptians even hunted the hippo, which was probably the largest and most dangerous animal in Egypt. They used long harpoons and lassoes. Like the lion, it was hunted almost to extinction.

BANQUETS

The big festivals were religious and they were organized by the priests of particular temples. Images of the gods were carried in procession and there was music, dancing, acrobats, jugglers, and feasts and banquets with a great deal of wine. *"Give me 18 cups of wine . . ."* said one, *"My inside is dry as straw."*

Everyone joined in the festivals, but richer people entertained their friends privately as Nebamun does here. His servants offer fresh lotus flowers to the guests and bowls of wine from the jars under the tables.

Story-telling was popular when the weather was cold. There were exciting tales of magic, ghosts and adventure. One story, the Shipwrecked Sailor, was rather like Sinbad. Cinderella is an Egyptian story too. You can still read these stories in translation today.

Many boys' games like wrestling, athletics, and gymnastics were individual trials of strength not team games. Girls sang and did acrobatic dances and some became professional musicians.

Senet board and pieces

BOARD GAMES

Senet and "Twenty squares" were played by everyone. Senet is often shown in tomb paintings to represent a game against death with the promise of eternal life for the winner. The aim was to get all your pieces off the board and to stop your opponent doing the same. Sticks, rounded on one side and flat on the other, were thrown and counted because the Egyptians did not have dice. This did not mean however that the Egyptians did not gamble!

WHAT·DID·THE·EGYPTIANS·WEAR?

In a hot country like Egypt clothes need to be light and cool. The basic fashion remained a short kilt for men and a simple shift dress for women, both woven from fine white linen. Later, elaborately pleated dresses and tunics became fashionable, worn with brightly colored jewelery and wide floral collars. Children and servants are usually shown naked, except for earrings or protective amulets. Egyptians were not embarrassed about their bodies and did not bother with underwear. In fact, the linen was so fine it was almost transparent.

PLAITING HAIR

In this carving on her coffin, Queen Kawit's maid plaits her hair. Both wear simple dresses held up by braces over the shoulder. The queen wears many bead necklaces, bracelets and anklets. Her mirror is made of polished bronze which gives nearly as good a reflection as glass. Poor women did not own mirrors and so used the reflection from water instead.

Mirror

Cosmetic scoop

Spatula

Bracelet

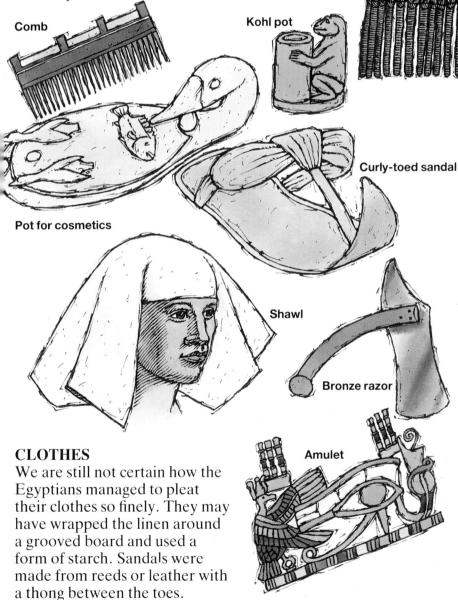

WIGS AND PERFUME

Elegant ladies at a banquet wore perfume cones on their wigs. As the evening passed, the sweet oily perfume would melt and run down over their dresses. Even servant girls had elaborate wigs and make-up.

Comb

Kohl pot

Pot for cosmetics

Curly-toed sandal

Shawl

Bronze razor

Amulet

HAIR

The Egyptians were not a naturally hairy people but often shaved their heads as well as their bodies. There was a brief fashion for pencil-thin moustaches but men really preferred to be clean-shaven. Children had shaved heads except for a side-lock called "the side-lock of youth", while their parents wore huge wigs in varying styles for special occasions. Surprisingly, wigs were comfortable and cool even in hot weather. The Egyptians thought the Greeks were very uncivilized because they had long hair and beards.

COSMETICS

As they had no soap, they used oil to soften the skin before shaving.

Ladies plucked their eyebrows and used cleansing creams and body scrubs, as well as lipstick and rouge made from red ochre.

CLOTHES

We are still not certain how the Egyptians managed to pleat their clothes so finely. They may have wrapped the linen around a grooved board and used a form of starch. Sandals were made from reeds or leather with a thong between the toes.

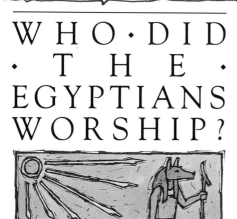

Religion played a central part in Egyptian life. It helped people to understand the world around them and to cope with the difficulties of everyday living. They also had a strong belief in an even better after-life. The gods controlled everything. There were household gods to look after the family, local gods of the village and the great universal state gods worshipped on official occasions.

Most people had a small chapel in their garden or an altar inside their house. On festival days people went to the state temples, although they were not allowed beyond the first courtyard. The inner part of the temple was sacred and only the priests were allowed there. Hymns like this were sung:

"Hail to you Amun, Maker of mankind
God who created all beings, Great and goodly king."

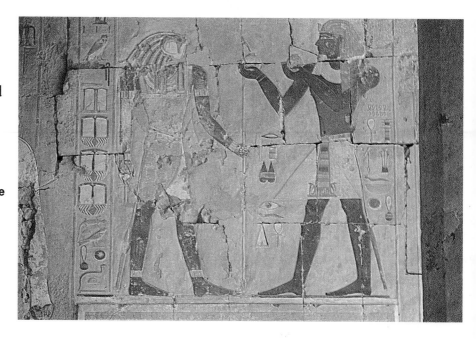

OFFERINGS

Here the Pharaoh is making an offering to the god, who protected him as he protected his people. One of the king's titles was "Son of Ra", the sun god. The sun god was the most important god of all. In earlier times the Pharaoh himself was thought to become a god when he became king. In death he became one with Osiris, the god of death and rebirth.

1 Montu – god of war
2 Amun – Creator god
3 Thoth – god of writing and knowledge
4 Khons – god of the Moon
5 Horus – Royal protector
6 Sekhmet – goddess of war
7 Sobek – crocodile god
8 Anubis – god of the Necropolis
9 Isis – goddess of women
10 Osiris – god of death and rebirth
11 Hathor – goddess of love

1   2   3   4   5

AMUN

These statues showing Pharaoh under the protection of Amun line the approach to the temple of Karnak. "The Hidden One" was a creator god who looked after both Egypt and the king.

GODS

There were many families of gods, each consisting of a husband, wife and their child, who were associated with special animals or birds. Hathor, goddess of love, has a cow's ears and horns. Cows were thought to be very beautiful animals. Sobek has the head of a crocodile.

Many people believed in magic too. Children wore special amulets or charms to protect them against evil or any illness. There were love potions and spells for almost everything, including not being eaten by a crocodile or not entering the next life on your head!

6   7   8   9   10   11

DID · THE EGYPTIANS ·BELIEVE·IN· ·LIFE·AFTER· · DEATH ? ·

Life here on earth was so good that the Egyptians wanted it to last forever. As that was impossible they believed the next life was even better and spent a great deal of time and effort preparing their "house of eternity" or tomb. It was very important to preserve the physical body too, so they developed the art of mummification or embalming. To destroy the physical body was to lose eternal life.

BURIALS

Early burials like the one on the left were very simple. This body is over 5,000 years old, but you can still see some of the man's hair as the hot sand has preserved his body so well. Once bodies were put into wooden coffins it needed more than sand to preserve them.

MUMMIFICATION

Internal organs such as the lungs, liver and intestines were removed from the body, as well as the brain, but the heart was usually left in. The body was packed in natron (a compound of sodium) for about forty days. Once it had dehydrated, it was washed, annointed with spices, and wrapped in linen bandages. Eventually, the wrappings became more elaborate and complex than the real body.

MOURNING

All the family went to the funeral. Servants carried furniture, clothes and offerings of food and drink into the tomb, while paid mourners wailed and put dust on their heads in sorrow. This still happens in Egyptian villages. It was very important for the owner's name to be painted on the coffin, for *"to speak the name of the dead is to make him live again"*.

AFTER DEATH

Nothing could stop tomb robbers hunting for gold and jewels. By 1000 BC all known royal tombs had been robbed. Every person had a physical body, a double or in Egyptian a *Ka*, and a spirit (shown as a human-headed bird), or in Egyptian a *Ba*. On the coffins the faces are always shown as young and beautiful.

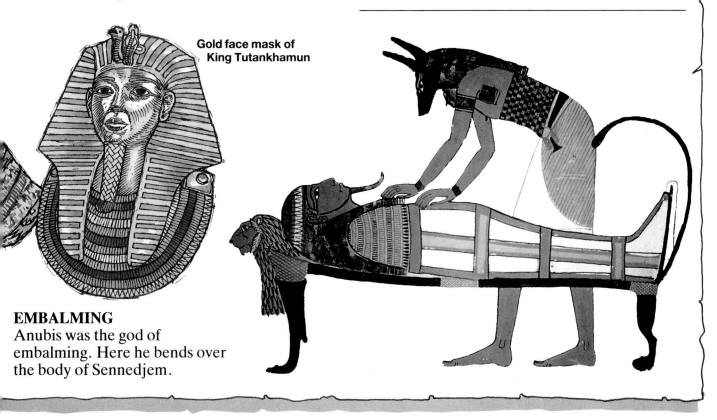

Gold face mask of King Tutankhamun

EMBALMING

Anubis was the god of embalming. Here he bends over the body of Sennedjem.

Egypt was owned by one man – the Pharaoh. The whole land was his garden and he cultivated it. That was the theory, but in reality he had an enormous number of officials and administrators to make sure the government ran smoothly. Egyptian society was like a pyramid from the king at the top, the viziers and officials in the middle and the peasants at the bottom.

At different periods in history the Pharaoh was thought of as a god himself, as the son of the sun god, as a "Good Shepherd" looking after his flock, and as a great warrior defeating all his enemies. He literally trod them underfoot as the soles of his sandals were decorated with images of his captives.

RAMESSES II
This Pharaoh ruled for over 60 years and was responsible for some of the greatest buildings in Egypt, like the temple of Abu Simbel. One statue of him is over 23 feet high.

THE PRIESTHOOD
The king made offerings to the gods and in return they protected him and the land of Egypt. However, it was the priests who actually made the offerings. In return they received land, wealth and tax-exemptions. Eventually, the priests grew more powerful than their king and really ruled Egypt in all but name. Priests could also be civil servants and military commanders.

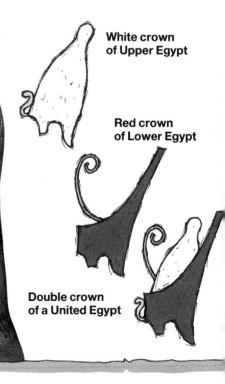

White crown of Upper Egypt

Red crown of Lower Egypt

Double crown of a United Egypt

AMENOPHIS

Amenophis, son of Hapu, was overseer of all the King's Works. He lived to be over 80 and became the most important non-royal person in the land. He is shown as a scribe, but he was also an architect and a military official.

OFFICIALS

We know of many instructions on how to be a good ruler:

"Promote your officials and pay them well
So they will not be tempted to take bribes
Great is the great man whose great men are great.
Strong is the king who has councillors.
Do not prefer the well-born to the commoner.
Choose a man on account of his ability."

It seems very sensible advice. Both good administrative skills and bravery in battle were well rewarded, and commoners could be promoted to high office.

The painting below shows the cattle count of Nebamun (the man hunting on page 24). Every two years a census was taken for tax. Egypt was a very bureaucratic land and employed many tax officials.

 NAMES

Pharaoh means "Great House", like saying palace or The White House.

Every king had five names. We use the fifth name, but the Egyptians used the fourth. For example, Nebkheprure Tutankhamun.

WERE·THE EGYPTIANS ARTISTS?

Although we have found so many monuments and tombs we know the names of hardly any Egyptian artists. They did not sign their work and were thought of as "craftsmen" rather than "artists". Artists drew what they knew to be there and not what they actually saw. Art had to last forever so they drew ideal views and hardly ever showed faults or emotions. Most of this art was sealed in the tombs, but we do know that they also painted their own houses, including floors and ceilings, in bright colors.

DRAWING

Drawing was an extension of writing. Human figures were living hieroglyphs. Before painting, a squared grid was prepared in red paint to make certain that the proportions of the figure were correct. A human figure measured 18 squares from top to toe. Egyptian artists looked at the world in a very special way. They drew what they knew to be there not what they actually saw. This means that they hardly used perspective like the Greeks. They put their subject at the center of the picture and not themselves.

SENEB'S FAMILY

Seneb was the chief valet and royal tutor. Here he is shown with his family. Look how the artist has made the two children tiny and put them in place of Seneb's legs.

PHARAOH TUTHMOSIS III

A wooden drawing board marked out with a grid for the seated figure of Pharaoh Tuthmosis III.

The picture on the right shows how skilful the Egyptians were in using gold. This is the back of Tutankhamun's throne – the blue lapis lazuli is inlaid into the gold. In the wallpainting below another couple are shown side by side in their tomb. All the colors used were made from natural materials:

Black   *carbon/charcoal*
White   *gypsum/calcium carbonate*
Red   *ochre/iron oxide*
Blue   *copper/lapis lazuli*
Green   *copper chloride compound*
Glue   *egg white*

The artist skilfully covers the uneven ceiling with trailing vines and bunches of grapes.

STONE AND GOLD

Architecture was also thought of as art and we do know the name of one of the world's first architects, Imhotep who you can read more of on page 38. The Egyptians were the first people in the world to build in stone. Their kings were buried in pyramids. By the time Tutankhamun died, the pyramids were already 2000 years old and were a popular tourist attraction. We are lucky enough to have his gold death mask. Because he was such an unimportant king, his little tomb was buried underneath a much bigger one.

DID·THE EGYPTIANS LIKE·MUSIC?

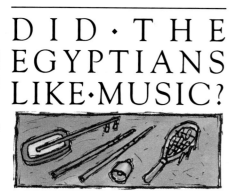

The Egyptians liked popular music, dancing, story-telling and poetry. Professional musicians were hired, along with dancing girls, for the entertainment at banquets.

There was no theater as we know it and no organized circuses, but many dramas told popular stories about the gods. These were performed at the great festivals in the temple and we can read the texts carved on the walls.

SONGS AND DANCE

Below is another scene from Nebamun's banquet. The musicians are female and are as fashionably dressed as the guests, with the latest earrings from Syria. They play the double flute and mark time for the dancers with castenets while singing about the beauties of nature.

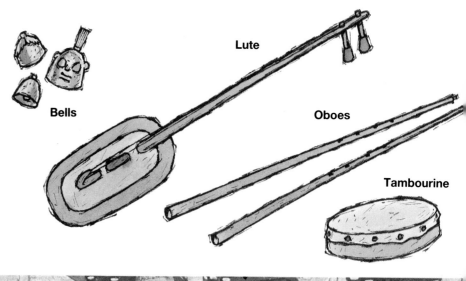

Bells

Lute

Oboes

Tambourine

MUSICAL INSTRUMENTS

Time was kept by clappers and tambourines, while the orchestra played flutes, double clarinets, lyres and harps which might be as tall as the musicians! We are not quite sure what the music sounded like as no notation has been found, but it probably had a strong rhythm and was easy to dance to. Ceremonial trumpets were found in Tutankhamun's tombs, but most of our information has to come from paintings. Blind people were sometimes shown as professional musicians and they were probably story-tellers as well.

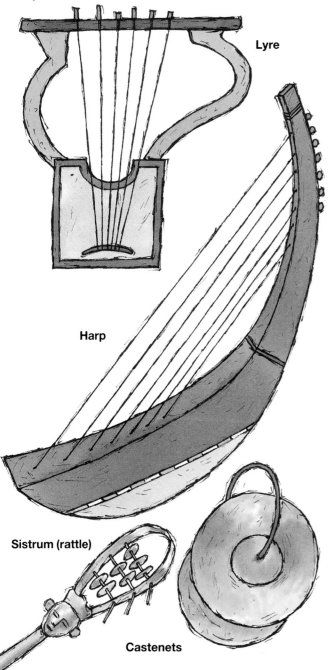

Lyre

Harp

Sistrum (rattle)

Castenets

BES

Bes, the dwarf god, is often shown dancing as he was a friendly, happy god who looked after the home and family.

Singing and dancing were part of everyday life in the fields, at work and at home.

A BANQUET SONG

These lines reminded everyone how good life was:

"Follow your heart as long as you live . . .
Wailing saves no one from the pit . . .
Make a holiday
Don't be weary
No one can take his wordly goods with him
None who departs this life comes back again."

DANCE

Dancing was part of both religious and popular music. Acrobats took part in temple processions, but at private banquets more graceful dancers were preferred. Many dancers could sing and play at the same time.

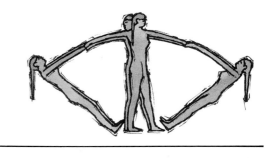

·WERE·THE· EGYPTIANS INVENTORS?

ARCHITECTS
The Egyptians were skilled architects and surveyors and used a standard unit of measurement called the royal cubit, about 20 inches. To make sure all surfaces were straight and level, they used the right angle and plumb level. If the surface is flat, the level bisects the right angle. The plumb level makes sure that the vertical surfaces are correct.

The Egyptians were very practical people. They were not very interested in new ideas if old ones worked perfectly well. Much of their technology was developed early in their history, especially in the fields of engineering and mathematics. Everything was referred back to "the time of the gods" (the beginning of things), and so progress and invention were not encouraged, unless they solved particular problems. Other countries eventually became more technologically advanced than Egypt and she was defeated by people with more sophisticated weapons of iron. This was the one major mineral that Egypt lacked. But both the Greeks and the Romans learned many things from the Egyptians, who were skilled astronomers, architects, builders, doctors and dentists.

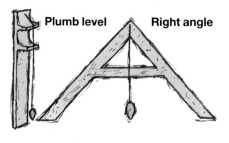

Plumb level   Right angle

PYRAMIDS
The pyramid designed by Imhotep had stepped sides, but architects soon developed the true pyramid. Unfortunately the white limestone outer casing of the pyramids seen here was stolen and used to build the city of Cairo.

TRANSPORTING STONE

Heavy blocks of stone were dragged on sledges pulled by oxen or men. It took 172 men to move a statue over 23 feet high and weighing 60 tons. One man pours water on the ground to make the sledge runners move more easily while the foreman beats time and the workmen sing.

Stone slab being pulled up a hill on a sled

OBELISK

The obelisk on the left was cut from a single block of granite. It is 97 feet high, weighs 323 tons and took 7 months to cut from the quarries at Aswan on the orders of Queen Hatshepsut.

MEASURES

◯ means part.

So ◯ = ⅕.

½ was written ⊏

So ⅓ + ½ was ◯ ⊏

There are over two million blocks of stone in the Great Pyramid, each weighing over 2½ tons.

Quarrymen were issued with bread, vegetables and two linen garments per month.

In the nineteenth century ancient Egyptian obelisks were taken away and set up in London, Paris, Rome and New York.

MAKING PLANS

"I built the gods' temples and I excavated a pool before them adorned with lotus blossom" said one king. Skilled architects made plans before building so that every tomb and temple was correctly calculated mathematically. Plans like the one below were used.

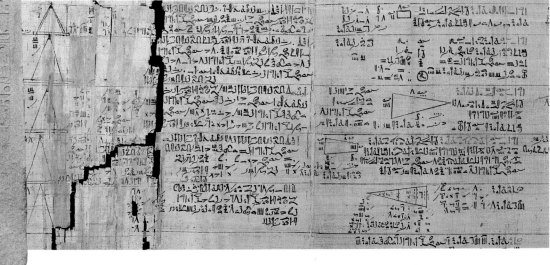

DID · THE EGYPTIANS TRAVEL ABROAD ?

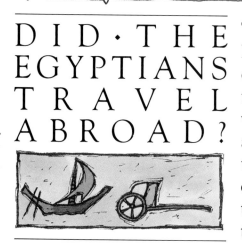

BOATS

Most boats were not heavy, sea-going vessels but transport barges, grain ships or simple sailing boats, sometimes made of papyrus reeds. Cedar wood imported from Lebanon was made into large boats used for special ceremonies and occasions.

The Egyptians did not need roads as the Nile was their highway. Except for short journeys on foot or donkey, everything moved by boat. Some people probably never traveled further than the next village although everyone who could afford it tried to make a pilgrimage to Abydos, a great religious center, at least once in their life. Officials traveled on government business collecting taxes and overseeing the courts of justice. Rich landowners visited their various estates. The whole royal court moved from the civil capital, Memphis, to Karnak for religious festivals. Many royal ladies also had palaces there.

But Egyptians did not really like leaving their own land. Foreigners were regarded as rather inferior, and abroad was full of unknown dangers. You might die there and be buried by strangers. It was better to stay at home if you could.

Old Kingdom
Egyptian boat

EXPLORERS

It was Nubia (which means "gold") and the south that attracted explorers and traders. One man even brought back a pygmy as a gift for the Pharaoh. Expeditions were difficult and dangerous. They brought back ebony and ivory, gold and skins and even monkeys and live panthers.

The word "to sail" means "to go south".

"Downstream" is "to go north".

Boats sailed south with the wind and drifted north with the current.

When they discovered the River Euphrates in Asia, the Egyptians called it "the up-side down river" as it ran the opposite way to the Nile.

Camels were hardly used until Roman times.

SEMITE TRADERS

Egypt also traded with the East. Below are Semites from Syria coming to trade. They needed permission from the customs to cross the border. Their brightly colored clothes, leather boots and beards are quite different from anything the Egyptians knew. You can see that they even brought their furniture with them. These foreigners seemed so strange that their visit was carefully recorded in a tomb painting. You can see some of the objects Egypt imported. There was little need for Egyptians to travel.

DID · THE EGYPTIANS HAVE · AN · ARMY ? ·

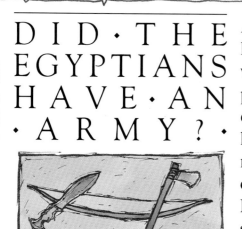

A Pharaoh boasted that he could mobilize the entire land. There were records of every person so conscription was easy in time of war. But Egypt did not need a professional army for a very long time. The sea and the desert protected the country from invasion. The king had his own bodyguard and troops raised by local nobles if necessary. As other lands became powerful and envious of Egypt's wealth, a professional army developed. Mercenaries were also used, especially as police and security guards.

Soldiers carried a spear and raw-hide shield. Later came body armor, battle axes and a short, stabbing dagger. The main infantry used bows with bronze or flint-tipped arrows.

CAVALRY

By the time of Tutankhamun (about 1350 BC) horses and chariots formed an élite cavalry corps. Horses had been introduced from Asia about 300 years earlier and all technical terms were of foreign origin. The chariots were light and maneuverable and carried two soldiers – one steering and the other shooting. There were many complaints of young men driving their chariots too fast just to impress their friends.

VICTORY

Below is a scene from a painted box which belonged to Tutankhamun. The king is defeating the Asians who are in complete disorder while his troops are in neat ranks behind him! He wears the blue war crown, body armor and a wrist guard, and is shown without his charioteer.

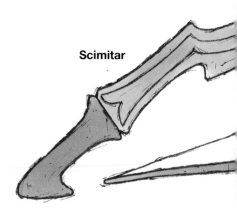

Scimitar

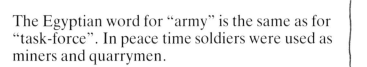

The Egyptian word for "army" is the same as for "task-force". In peace time soldiers were used as miners and quarrymen.

The first battle in world history that we can reconstruct was the Battle of Kadesh in 1285 BC between Egypt and the Hittites. Both sides claimed to have won.

The army was divided into 4 divisions of 5,000 men. Each bowman carried about 30 arrows.

Bronze dagger

Bow and quiver

Axe

WARFARE

The Egyptians preferred to rule by influence rather than war, but if that was impossible then they showed little mercy. Prisoners often had one hand cut off so they could not fight again and their families were made slaves. Many battles are shown on the outside of temple walls, including the famous Battle of Kadesh. The Egyptians are always shown in neat ranks, while their enemies are completely disorganized. These scenes were useful propaganda to persuade the people that Egypt was always the winner. Sometimes they were offered freedom in return for fighting for Egypt, and many former enemies retired with a grant of land. Egypt never had a true empire and did not colonize other countries but many cities in Syria and Palestine owed allegiance to Egypt. Eventually Egypt was invaded by the Persians, the Greeks and then the Romans to become part of their empire.

SPEARMEN OF MESERHETI

These are private soldiers of an official. In the Middle Kingdom it was common to put miniature models in the tomb. Meserheti was obviously very proud of his spearmen.

· GLOSSARY ·

ASWAN DAM The first dam was built in 1898 to control the annual flood. The new dam was opened in 1972. Behind it is Lake Nasser – 310 miles long. Most of the old land of Nubia is under this lake.

ABU-SIMBEL These temples were rediscovered in the 19th century. They were cut in the cliff-face in about 1269 BC.

BA Often translated as "soul" and shown as a human-headed bird. The *Ba* could move outside the tomb and return to earth.

CUBIT A measure of length of about 17¾ inches. A royal cubit was 20½ inches. It was the distance from the elbow to the top of the middle finger. 1 cubit = 6 palms or 24 digits.

DYNASTY A 3rd century BC historian divided the different ruling families of Egypt into 32 dynasties.

HIEROGLYPH This is a Greek word meaning "sacred writing on stone". It was used for official inscriptions on monuments rather like our printing. Some signs were pictures but some had a sound value as well as a pictorial one. There was also an alphabet of 24 consonants, as vowels were not written.

KA A person's double who stayed with them after death. It was the *Ka* who received the offerings of food and drink in the tomb.

KOHL An eye cosmetic made from malachite and later galena or lead sulphide.

MISTRESS OF THE HOUSE Title given to married ladies.

MORTUARY TEMPLE Each Pharaoh built a temple as well as a tomb. This was where the remembrance services and rituals were performed by the priests.

NATRON Sodium carbonate found in the Egyptian desert and used in embalming.

NECROPOLIS Greek word meaning "city of the dead". Used for a burial place or cemetery.

OBELISK A long square tapering shaft with a little pyramid on top. The name is from the Greek meaning "needle". They were one of the symbols of the sun and were usually put up in pairs outside temples or tombs.

PAPYRUS A tall plant belonging to the sedge family. It was once common in Egypt but now is no longer found. It was used to make papyrus rolls which the Ancient Egyptians wrote upon. The longest roll found so far is 134 feet long and is in the British Museum.

PYRAMID Built either of stone or brick. Pyramids were intended as tombs. All pyramids were robbed in ancient times and we shall never know what treasures they once held.

SPHINX A mythical animal with the body of a lion and the face of a man. The most famous one guards the pyramids at Giza.

VALLEY OF THE KINGS For about 500 years from 1500 BC the Pharaohs chose to be buried in a remote valley opposite Thebes. Their tombs were hidden deep in the cliffs where it was hoped robbers would not find them. Some of the queens and princes were buried in a nearby valley called the *Valley of the Queens*.

VIZIER The highest government official. By the New Kingdom there were 2 viziers – one at Memphis in the north and one at Thebes in the south.

· I N D E X ·